Her
Poetic
Rise

Books by the Anonymous Author and Artist

Life's Short Stories

Fictional characters vie to live their own lives.

Life's Mixed Poetry

Poems are mixed schematically, stylistically, and randomly.

Life's Novellas: Fate Waits Upon No One

The good and the bad are juxtaposed, chronologically, fictionally, and theatrically.

Their Poetic Minds

Poems are juxtaposed, religiously, femininely, and dichotomously.

Poems of Life

Poems are mixed schematically, stylistically, and randomly.

Life's Heart Break: A Novella

In the end, will Zenald discover what may be one of life's biggest heart-breaks: heart-ache?

Duty & Destruction I

A real female experiences life in and out of the U.S. military.

Life's Poetic Dichotomies

Some of life's biggest dichotomies are juxtaposed poetically.

Art Book

The Diamond & Heart Art Collections

Pictures are exhibited, categorically, by coloring schemes and coloring mediums; all of which, have been affected with special effects.

Schemes: pastel shades; earth tones; primary colors; gray, black and white; black and white.

Mediums: colored pencils; water coloring; pastel coloring; acrylic coloring; oil coloring.

Her
Poetic
Rise

Anonymous

Century Conquests

Her Poetic Rise

Copyright © 2010 by Anonymous

www.centuryconquests.com
info@centuryconquests.com

ISBN: 978-0-9850698-2-7

First Printing: Spring 2010

Century Conquests' rev. date: 09/01/10

Cover graphic designed by: Century Conquests © 2011

Century Conquests ® 2012

Her
Poetic
Rise

Anonymous

Acknowledgements

For the small voice deep in me that still wants me to carry on poetically.

I thank everyone, as well, that have helped with the publication of this book.

I even thank every reader of my book, for permitting me the privilege:
to liven up—you, and hold your interest, and even inform you.

Author's Note

Withstanding its extended products or services or even the lack there of, this book was published, previously, by a so-called "Subsidy Publisher, or Vanity Publisher"; whose book cover and interior both were different than this book's.

This book has been redesigned, revised, and republished—since, under the direction of a brand new entity.

Sith Cynthia is ascended to that rest
Of endless joy and true Eternitie,
That glorious place that cannot be exprest
By any wight clad in mortalitie,
In her almightie love so highly blest,
And crown'd with everlasting Sov'raigntie;
       Where Saints and Angells do attend her Throne,
       And she gives glorie unto God alone….

—Aemilia Lanyer, *Salve Deus Rex Judaeorum*
       (1569-1645)

Preface

Her rise has almost always been forthcoming.

Whose sin was the very greatest, Eve's or Adam's—woman's or man's? That the Prince of Sinners seduced Eve, so unknowingly; into flavoring fruit from the forbidden tree; right, in the "Garden of Eden," seemed to be a lesser sin. On, the other hand, Adam, indeed, knew that such fruit was forbidden—or, sinful; still, he accepted it from Eve and then flavored the fruit, him-self. This very fundamental comparison of liability was what so precipitated, and then perpetuated a particular woman's claim: to elevation, or status, and stature. But, it was not enough, ever.

For, She needed more than just biblical proof that Woman was not liable for the collapse of the human race. She necessitated the words and ways of God; to lessen Her regression; to lessen Her repression; to lift Her from oppression; to put Her right into *freedom*, or liberation. However, three other things were needed to truly effectuate her rise from de-elevation: commitment, courage, and honor; all of which just had to secure her a great measure of heroism. Or, better, fame, and, power, and even, honor, and not necessarily in such chronological order, all went together; likewise, to effectuate a great measure of heroism—or, boldness, for the Woman of a Lady.

Hence, the past brought along a person of such character. That, the King and the Queen of Destiny both, just, saw fit for her to occupy a very special place in history, so particularly, in literary history. What was equally important was the era in which this heroic person came to illustriousness. It was also during the Renaissance, and the reign of King James Stuart (1603-1649), that one's mentality and one's personality both were influenced, heavily; right, by the very religious, cultural, social, and, political, and, even, economical influences, or existent powers.

It was, too, through out such era that the Woman attained liberation and literary greatness, or illustriousness, by just having been her-self. Aemilia Lanyer (1569-1645), or this Poetess, and precursory, if not prodigious Female of a Feminist, was appointed solely by the Queen of Queens; and, even, was appointed solely by the King of Queens and Kings, to just navigate an utterly un-charted territory. The zone was none other than femininity. Lanyer went about her work with super steely resolve. She plotted the course of feminine liberation by using several literary techniques right in her writings: mainly, the words and ways of God. For, His ways and words fitted quite well with her poetry and prose—or, fantastically, if not fabulously feministic point-of-view.

Moreover, and, very interestingly, enough, Aemilia Lanyer's poetic counter-part, or the Jacobean meta-physician, John Donne (1572-1631), attained illustriousness; or, he attained literary greatness, as well, by just having been him-self. Still, the two illustrious poets, almost, certainly, sought, to integrate their in-corporeal and corporeal selves into one. A mind, heart, body, and soul—or one, that, almost, always, sought, to obtain, and retain, and even maintain a very delicate balance of being true; to some higher principles other than one's very own self-imposed principles of life and methodologies of living it. Because John Donne often sought such in vain, which brought about and then reinforced his dichotomously poetic point-of-view, (or pain), as seen in his clever conceits; he did not find the same sort of peace in life so un-like Aemilia Lanyer.

His utter ulterior reasoning for having written both poetically and dichotomously seemed to have been all about exposing the double-sidedness of characters; The process of having made comparisons between essentially different things, or notions, via utterly un-paralleled imagery, and manipulation of words, or even dichotomous images. Most, undoubtedly, Aemilia Lanyer found the Supreme Goodness' force or power right in her poetry. Contrastingly, John Donne found such power or force in his poetry or the idea of it, confusing, at best, or worst, definitely, and dichotomously damning. Such dichotomy (ies) is/are seen in the dichotomous poems of the poetry books that are entitled *Life's Poetic Dichotomies*, and *Their Poetic Minds*, respectively. A circularly or a conversely contrastive comparison of the two poetic writers' brand of writing, quite, poetically, is interesting, and, incredibly.

Having been born, subsequently, right, to inferiority—but, not despondency, or crudity; Aemilia Lanyer began her poems in earnest—and, with very deep respect, when addressing her subjects. When Lanyer showed this sense of decorum, right away, such not only added to her credibility; but, also, she assumed a position equal to the addressee of her poems. It was, too, Lanyer's sure scope—or, aim, to elevate Herself right into the company of esteemed Ladies. Once, there, at the addressee's level, the addresser went on to bid them both good will and good support. Even, after having elevated herself right alongside her addressee, Lanyer still needed to seize the addressee's utterly un-divided attention. One of several tools that she used, as well, was to just emphasize and then capitalize most words, which could have been personified, so, femininely. Her absolute ability to have just stressed if not stretched—all, that just might have been so feminine; such allowed Lanyer to add some substance to the content, and frame the context of her poems, rather delicately.

She just continued to personify—or, to characterize the words in her poetry. That so capitalized on her circularly calculating course of discourse if not recourse. She even proceeded to elevate women by twisting around biblical words and biblical references. This religious purpose served, absolutely, as an authoritative means: To place Women right on various pedestals that both God and Christ have since seen fit for them to just occupy. She continued to inculcate in the minds of women, and specifically—that, they just had to fight, (and, with their entire might), for what was so right, or theirs. To take considerable consolation in just knowing that the utterly un-pretty price of persecution for women has been paid, already, by Christ. And, sometimes, the highest price was paid when women remained so roundly impregnable. They were un-willing, and, utterly, to bend—or, yield, or, even, lower their standards; when, especially, having been opposed by men. The women much preferred to give their lives, instead.

Once, a woman, consequently, assumed a very high position in a social class, or a political system, or even something else; hence, a most meaningful measure of support served—only, to enforce her strength, right, there. This was why, and, so obviously, that Aemilia Lanyer often brought together marvelously mythological Goddesses in very varied verses and very varied scenes; whose attributes were exactly what women needed to maintain their nakedly new-fangled power and far more. For, the masculine qualities having been so associated with men—(or, so-called Gods—or, Deities), existed, now, in the women that so seized the power. These women of pretty powerful senses were given, even, additional tools of the trade by the Queen of Queens, like, great sensibility.

Another very factual form of support for a woman was the reflection that she saw whilst looking at a mirror. It was her image, there, that needed to reflect, and, roundly, commitment, courage, and honor; all of which so sustained the lady as she, the reflector, went about her bid for permanent liberation. When Lanyer told the women in her poems to look deeply at their mirrors, she was saying: Now, here is what you-all can be. You-all—the reflectors ought not to doubt your-selves or hesitate to become all that you-all can be. Such words were meant, quite simply, for every single woman; who just dared to look at some mirror and then proclaimed her own self—*so free*, of some terribly tired tyranny.

More, who were the tyrants? That oppressed a woman with brand spanking new commitment, and courage, and even honor to rise way above oppression? They were so-called Kings, Judges, and any despotic person. It was, also, the King's men that Aemilia Lanyer liked to compare with and then contrast to women. Rarely, if ever, did she refer to any mortal or male figures—except, to argue right against them in support of some Female's superiority. She spoke single-mindedly, and candidly, about their lowness and sometimes about her own lowness. But, nothing affected Lanyer more than the existent power structure. The fantastically flagrant in-equality that existed between Woman and man fermented a deep-seated wrath in her spirit—or, soul. So, right, through the ups and downs of both personal and professional woes; so, rightly, She simply sought literary discourse as a means to equalize the genuine difference in gender, in the arts. In having done so, Lanyer achieved a very delicate balance of blending religion and feminism.

She emphasized, most passionately, the absolutely authoritative words and ways of God and Christ as the boldly beauteous backdrop of her poetry and prose. Their ways and words almost certainly concretized her speaking and writing, so poetically. It is, too, the mark of a very great Woman, who has the commitment, courage, and honor; to see her deliciously, or her decidedly good dream(s) realized, without doubt, or fail: To over-come gender-barriers, which may facilitate another Woman's claim to honor, and power, and even fame. No matter what her status or stature in life may be. Most, fabulously, "The Feast," that Lanyer often referred to was none other than Herself, and an event so celebrating her very nakedly *noble* cause. Thus, in the end, Aemilia Lanyer's sure scope of influence—or, power; as it were, was not just in the substance of Her character—but, even, in the power of Her powerfully pretty pen.

Lastly, it is all through the use of my very own pretty pen—or, pretty pencil, that I have created the poems in this poetry book, similarly, to Aemilia Lanyer's feministic point-of-view. Or, better yet, to have done so—right, in the spirit of what the advocator advocated for, right, through the use of different types of rhymes or, a blend thereof: masculine—bows/knows; feminine—chances/dances; slant—branches/dances; perfect—flowery/showery; and, rhyme schemes—aa, aba, abab, ababa, and so on; and, kinds of poems: couplets—aa, bb, cc, dd…; terza rimas—aba, bcb, cdc, ded…; quatrains—abab, cdcd, efef, ghgh…; whose difference in stanzas, (or lines), right, in connection with the diverse rhyme schemes are, to a great extent, sonnets: a mixture of the classic 14 lines of poetry, as seen right in the Spenserian sonnet: abab, bcbc, cdcd, ee; Petrarchan (Italian) sonnet: abbaabba, cdecde; Shakespearean sonnet: abab, cdcd, efef, gg.

Right, through out the use of such poetic mechanisms, the poems are just set to a regular form versus an irregular form. The first—regular, is similar to a sonnet and the second—irregular, is similar to free verse. I have created, supplementarily, a feminine, or a very feministic point-of-view—(*P.O.V.*) with respect to the poems. That so includes capitalization, personification, feminization, and, elevation, and even, liberation—or, de-masculinization, and so forth. All will come right together, to some extent, at last. As, to exemplify, if not personify a Woman's rise from lowness to a state of highness: Right, with the use of the Creator's words, ways, and all, in one form, or another form, or even some other form.

Her Highness

By the grace of the Most High;

She arises from the depths of both deep dark gloom and deep dark doom:

BOOM!

Like, a pink, pretty, palpable, and powerful, and even perfect flower that's *now* in full

BLOOM!

A.

Part I

An Enthusiast

Because of God's words and ways, the Woman seeks to yoke Hope,

Only, to find out that it almost certainly can be chok'd—or, rop'd.

Castle Builder

Because of her faith in God Almighty, she's nev'r touched by Despair;

Like the feminine Big Foot, that cares everything for being His would-be heir (ess).

True-Hearted

To make her fate come true, the woman always has hope, Faith, and ambition, and even strength, or staying power, *personal power*:

    Persisting right in the merciful face of postponement;

    Because of the Lord's words—alone, she'll become the woman of the hour.

Tried and True

Being fulfill'd, her lot in life is almost nev'r in Doubt,

Tolerating its total and testimonial tout;

It almost always amounts to peace, piety, and power—or, her lot in life.

This is why she can't and won't stop—ev'r, from being devotedly devout.

Get Up and Go

On the job, the group of Females has lots of Ambition.

Nor are they ev'r scared by their fabulously fine femininity;

It almost nev'r causes them any vacillation.

This is to say—that, feminine qualities just aren't allowed to bring about any

Susceptibility.

Clock Watchers

At home, the hard-working wives are far more than slackers, tolerating hardly any Slack;
Their husbands will ev'n attest to such fact.

When they're not at home, the wives almost nev'r have to be fetched.

For other men already know that they can't or won't ev'r be snatched.

Will Power

In her Father's words, she seizes Might,

    Seizing that which almost nev'r gets away;

Because, the power of His words and ways always greaten the width,

    Widening up and down and around, all day;

        Hence, her strength only expands way pass its initial length.

Hole in One's Armor

In the Devil's starkly dark world, the woman nev'r struggles with Weakness;

For her ethics, morality, and character are all cement'd in the Supreme Goodness'

Righteousness.

In other words, no amount of darkness can ev'r blanket her bright world—or,

Lightness;

Plus, she just goes on lighting it (brightness) with such keen deepness.

Part II

Laying Away

Early on, the female learned the face-value of investment, or Commitment.

And, if any real deal proved, later, to have been un-timely,

It was her choice, solely, to still honor such agreement.

No Breach of Trust

At church, the Lady swears off all un-Chastity;
When, she's not at church, just the same, that she indulges whole-heartedly in celibacy or, Virginity.

Firmness of Mind

In the end, the female wins only because of her saintly Steadfastness.

In the beginning, though, her steady purpose in life seems un-prevailing.

She, still, manages, to prevail using her own special brand of pur-pos-ive-ness—or,

Stick-to-it-ive-ness.

Smarts

Being tir'd of zig-zagging—or, see-sawing—or, even, damn wig-wagging;

She'd nev'r dream of quitting or calling it Quits.

Since, she needs only to turn right around, rapidly, and religiously, yet again.

Given that, her brain is just over-flowing with wit.

Bold-Spiritedness

It's what propels the female to become a soldier—Valor;

    She'll be a fantastic fighter fighting ev'n before knowing its full consequence.

Such tour of duty will necessitate that her performance be rather stellar;

    Because, her pre-sparkling just like a super-star is almost always of great

Significance!

Strong Knees

HURRAH! She's raised herself to be far more than an utterly un-celestial Coward.
Therefore, the woman's future is almost nev'r sour as to make her glower and then
Cower.
She just looks to her beautifully bright future, willingly—spiritually, and is ready, most
steadily, to face it right down to the ground.
Also, the woman's bound—in-arguably, to nev'r be taken down like some weakling of a
damnably dark clown.

Part III

Self-Possession

Since the Girl has it within herself, she hardly ev'r seeks it while out and about:
Tranquility.

Shhhh!

Because, the Divine Being's teachings almost always appease her need for
Serenity.

Storm in a Teacup

At court, the woman is protect'd from any Turmoil;

She simply won't be foil'd or soil'd nor coil'd into anything that's not of His toil.

Fine Fettle

I almost always exercise to improve my Health.

    While exercising most unfailingly, I nev'r feel any wrath;

        But, instead, I've an abundance of my Divine Father's wealth.

Well-Being

Her schooling and training—or know-how is almost, always, enough, to keep it at bay,

Illness.

On guard, the female doctor is quite aware of her mis-diagnosis;

Whose male diagnostician has diagnosed her Backbone, mistakenly, and,

With great willfulness.

Heart's Desire

It'll find me on a gorgeous yet gray but great day—love—His Love:

Like, the gently snow-white-color'd bird that personifies piety and placidity—dove.

Then, it'll always want to stay with me and nev'r go away;

Such love doesn't want to go astray, ev'r, on any day; that may leave it at bay—and,

Not, at all, gay.

The Garden of Earthly Delights

The Lady nev'r desires it when it's un-available, Gratification.

She's simply content with the simple thought of knowing that it'll always be given to her
when need be;

      Thus, the Lady waits patiently and nev'r dreams of experiencing any fornication.

         Since, her religion will exact too damn high of a fee; for this, the Lady
can clearly see:

         That such sin will be seen—only, as a source of mortification;

      Or, seen, as a nakedly or a starkly and ev'n a damnably dark abomination!

No Heartache

The woman's beginning to adore the man that's causing her hardly any Heartbreak.

That, their love's proving to be steady yet somehow surrealistic but still real and

Spiritual—or, ev'n, destined.

This is why she always feels as if theirs is an utterly un-alterable relationship that's

Based solely on fate:

It's a rather dated and under-rated relation that needn't be jaded, ev'r, or

Tested.

Seventh Heaven

At work, the females almost nev'r experience any Pain;

HOORAH! It's because of their Maker's effort to keep them ache-less.

It's a small price, just, the same, that they won't have to pay for their

Super big gain.

Nor will they ev'r appear purpose-less;

Their Maker has ensur'd that the females' winnings will nev'r wane or be maim'd—

In vain.

High Spirits

When he's with the woman, the man feels such Joyfulness;

    When she feels him, he's no longer mask-less;

When the woman's with the man, he feels such jolliness;

    When she feels him, his spirit is that of vast-ness;

When he's not with the woman, the man just sinks into a state of impious coyness.

Well-Pleased

When she's with the man, the woman feels such Gayness.

When he touches her, she's no longer face-less.

When the man's with the woman, she nev'r feels any waywardness.

When he touches her, the woman's being is nev'r that of baseness.

When she's not with the man, she doesn't feel, at all, mate-less.

Stroke of Genius

BRAVO! The ingenious Boss-Lady has always earn'd her good Fortune.

Plus, she's nev'r thought once or twice or ev'n thrice about it having been hollow:

Staying on the go; traveling high and low; and, meeting folks that haven't been, at all,

Kosher.

Indeed, it's been a long and hard yet glorious trip that others have ev'n want'd to follow.

That's right; those same folks—or, fantastic fakers are nothing but vicious yet would-be

Vouchers.

Since, they've secretly want'd to steal if not kill the Boss-Lady's power.

No Mishap

Because of the Omniscient's gift to her, she almost nev'r encounter any Failure.

The firm's *V.I.P.'s* won't fail, ev'r, to hold her responsible or accountable while the female's at work.

      Since, it's the kind of responsibility and accountability that permits no blunder.

      If some type of fake error should happen, then, she needn't feel their ache.

As they alone—almost certainly, will've to bear the brunt of their own *damned*

                  Misjudgment;

Since any fake error is immunized, always, to the Omniscient's—or, His aptitude,

                  At any rate.

Forward Movement

WHOOPLA! The females can now flavor a very necessary break because of their most recent Gain.

Just the same, that they can take an ev'n bigger break since they won't have to ev'r back up:

Or, go back, to a time and a place, when their darkly naked beings are lived in a big, thick, and rusty chain.

They're not about to bear any, what so ev'r, utterly un-necessary pang that's akin to being in a roundly ruinous rut;

For sure, there'll be no more living in a damn hut—being caged, like some goddamn tame game whose very life is in vain.

Just, the same, that, they aim to take that very necessary break.

On break, the females will ev'n savor a big, sweet, and blissful piece of frostily chocolate cake! HOOPLA!

Win Over

In God's world, the woman takes whatev'r she needs or wants from life,

Bearing in mind that it'll cost;

Whose idyllic price is almost nev'r any Loss:

A pretty price so reasonably light that it won't weigh her down;

Beseeching Him to please take back that, which she's thus taken from life—or rather— found.

No matter how near such is to the ground, there'll be no pounding or day of reckoning;

As in His world, everything's done quite tactfully.

For, it's nev'r any kind of transgression,

By which the woman takes whatev'r she wants or needs from life;

Because, no price could or would ev'r cause her any strife.

Carried Away

At church, the girl feels such Joy,

     Feeling the Prime Mover's words flow right through her soul;

Its crux is no longer cold, neither can it ev'r be bought nor sold, so she's since been told,

     Feeling His words spur her super sensational spirit to soar.

At church—still, the girl wants to soar un-like some sluggishly wild boar,

     Feeling the Prime Mover just lift her spirit.

       Its crux rather full of joy that's a beautifully bright mirror;

     Seeing it toy with her light being that's now mirroring a morally up-right boy.

Great Times

It's almost nev'r about my joy or Sorrow;

Do I've too much of the former and not enough of the latter?

In either case, it's almost certain that the former—joy, will be right with me long after

Tomorrow.

It's, also, the latter, sorrow, whose colorless content fails to matter.

Is it at all feasible to have too much of the former and not enough of the latter?

In either case, it's almost certain that the latter is like a dark, deep, and dirty cellar—

Nev'r!

It's, also, the former, joy, whose substance is a pretty pious

Fella.

The last of which, sorrow—or, latter, that I can't and won't encounter—ev'r!

Part IV

Shaft of Light

It's what lightens the Woman in her darkest hour, Lightness;

For she's nev'r blind to the darkly debauch'd ways of man-kind, exhibiting maidenly

Mightiness.

Bright as Ink

It's what brightens the female's life, missing Darkness—or, un-failing Brightness.

Because of her saintly height, she's able to see what's ethically and morally right—

Day or night, without doubt or fail;

This is to say, that the light female's a real fighter and will nev'r be sightless.

Long on Looks

At church, the female worshiper's thoughts, words, and ways are all about Rightness.

She rises up in pretty pietistic prayer, crushing, circularly, the Monarch of Hell.

Whenev'r she departs it, church, the female's full of mightiness;

She just can't help but yell while being rescued from a devilishly jet-black jail—cell.

The worshiper intends, as well, to tell anyone who'll listen to her:

That, absolutely, nothing in the Absolute's world could or would ev'r make her fail:

Not ev'n, that fantastically Foul Fiend with that diabolically dark tail.

No Misdeed

Because of the woman's apt-ness, there's nev'r any space or place for Wrong-ness.

She's right, too, to always carry on the damn fight when her opponents try to out-do her.

Just the same, that her brilliancy is what, almost, always, causes the woman's alone-
ness.

That, she'd nev'r accept some man's overbearingly and destructively romantic dare;

There'll simply be no right and wrong or, a romantically mis-matched pair.

Since, she can't and won't jeopardize her super sweet soul-ness:

It's the only way if the woman ev'r hopes to remain, roundly, the Holy One's heir (ess).

That, she mustn't lose her way—stray; or, dip into dark-ness—low-ness,

By losing her bold-ness—or, holiness.

Big-Heartedness

At church, the Female pastor preaches Goodness,

     For it gives her an intense sense of fullness.

         At work, the pretty pastor ev'n takes pride in what's good;

It's easy to do so, because, she, almost, always, sports a moralistically righteous hood.

At court, all that isn't good nev'r saps the strength of her character, or chastity:

     It's the type of no-good that's still hooded with integrity or continuity.

         At church, once again, the female pastor just preaches away;

Because of her morality and purity whilst at work, church, and court—or play.

First-Class

At play, the class of women almost certainly is inoculat'd to any Badness,

   Living their lives both scrupulously and religiously;

      At the end of the day, it leaves them quite full of gladness.

In the viciously suspicious eyes of their men such is believ'd fictitiously;

   They're living their lives with strong, smart, and successful women.

   It leaves them, the women, in the end, nev'r sad but glad and deliciously.

In the sightless eyes of their men, they again can't and won't see their own starkly dark sin because they're sinners:

   Living their lives as darkly weak, dumb, and un-successful men;

Finally, it leaves the men utterly un-able to bend or mend—win, and then become a big bunch of winners.

Far-Sighted

The aged lady is thankful for her Saneness.

YIPPEE! It's almost certainly enough to keep her moving.

It's more than enough, also, to keep her from straying and remaining blameless.

Others, irreligiously, wish that she couldn't—wouldn't do such so coolly, or smoothly.

The same aged lady is ev'n more grateful for her soundness' loudness:

It's much easier to do her towing or sowing.

Others see such as an aged lady, whose life is that of utter un-soundness.

Still, she just loves to shout out—WOW!

It's because of the kow-towers—old and jealous and un-godly men—or others that like

Kow-towing.

They almost always in secret and invisibly bow to the aged lady;

Since her sanity is always here and nev'r gone by tomorrow.

It's only the great big bond between her pre-destined joy and her non-existent sorrow.

Steamed Up

The young woman's well attuned to her Madness;

It's quite enough to keep her coming and going.

Such ev'n leaves her roundly rosy cheeks with the color of redness.

That, she likes doing the Ruler of Heaven and Earth's wondrously wild sowing.

Doing so only in His world—or, in the in-corporeal world:

It's a beautifully big, bright, and right world where she once more likes towing.
However, some young men think—that, the young woman lives in an entirely different world;

That's a pretty pitch-dark, bushed, and confirmed cell: or, that, she's an overly oppressive mistress of some utterly un-holy Earl.

Never mind, too, that it's where she's always at home and nev'r alone.

From such jail—or cell, the young woman yells—that,
Everything in her world is well! Plus, it ev'n makes her long, thick, and red hair curl.
Nor does she ev'r imagine leaving such place of gold that'll nev'r mold or get old;

It's taken hold of the bold, young, and red-hot woman in a way that'll nev'r see her stray.

At least, this is what she's since been told.

Moving Force

HOORAY! The lovely pair of lovers loves living their Life.

The female lover, almost, certainly, considers herself a colorfully celestial catch.

And, their love almost nev'r causes either of them any strife.

It's just another sure sign that their love's a heavenly match;

The lovers' lot in life mandates as much:

That, neither of them ends up alone nor be an utterly un-lovable toad.

Just, the same, that the male lover trusts—that, all of life's toll roads will be pav'd with love and such.

The female lover ev'n trusts that such will nev'r turn to dark mold or get cold or ev'n grow old.

Plus, the lovers' love can only add warmth to such love.

It's lovability that always warms up the mere metal of their latch;

That the lovers, lovably, circularly, and conscientiously clasp.

Because of it—metallic fastener, the lovers almost always find themselves in the above.

To be sure, the pair of lovers' lovely love—or, match, has only just begun to hatch.

Yet again, the lovable pair of lovers loves living their life.

They just love each other while the female lover relishes being blessed beautifully.

Or, she's so very blessed to just be the love of the male lover's life or even his most heavenly wife.

Skull and Crossbones

No longer full of life, the fortunate Females are almost certainly ready for its end, Death.

Neither do they care about their fantastically fade-less star.

Forthrightly, the females are just eager to depart this un-godly Earth;

It's because of its utterly un-godliness, which keeps it way below par.

Oh, yes! They're thoroughly tired of being blamed:

Though, the females are blame-less for having gained the Eternal's flame—or, power.

Having been maimed, and after having endured such or much excruciating pain; they're totally through, being tamed.

The females have only blossomed into His great big bouquet of pink and pretty and palpable and powerful and even perfect flowers.

Such, in fact, has made some poor, puny, and power-less males—or chauvinists, holler.

Approaching the end or death, the females needn't flower their fortunes anymore.

Most powerfully, they've flowered enough to make those shallow, envious, and chauvinistic males steady wallow.

They'll just continue to waddle in a damnably dark sea of utter un-sanctity, galore.

Void of life, the fabulously fortunate females are now ready for its fabulous end.

For they've lived, quite unfailingly, such honorable lives that've been pretty free of sin.

An Awakening

It's what lightens an already bright tomb—the Renaissance—or, Her Re-Birth.

Such is ev'n entombed brightly in 24-carat-gold.

Mercifully, the Infinite's loosening His hold;

She's quite worthy of being let loose, again, to live in golden mirth.

But, will the woman again grace the starkly satanic planet of Earth?

It's a super stifling space, whose pretty poisonous place garners much mold.

And, no, she needn't be told:

That not ev'n 24-carat-gold can hold off such rot—or, decay, that'll only eat away at her
Worth.

Hence, the woman's joyously content to just grace another remote residence or home:

It's a gloriously light, and right, and ev'n mighty place—or space;

There, the Infinite's angles and saints will help abate all that's unearthly.

This is to say, that she won't ev'r think about "The Garden of Earthly Delights."

That's right; nev'r will the woman be left alone to just decay or rot.

That, you'll nev'r find her at home—alone, having since turned into an old, dark, heavy,
and moldy, and even an irreligious bone.

In other words, absolutely nothing in His world could or would ev'r make the
Woman turn deathly.

Like, a big, bright, and beautiful dot, it's just simply not her beautifully blest
Life's lot.

Rise and Shine

Why has their rise almost always been imminent?

Because, the Sovereign of the Universe has since said so:

His female dependents haven't just been sin-less but ev'n more than benevolent;

True, that the females have nev'r dreamt of falling to any old or new sort of low.

For, they've, almost, always, sought, to ingratiate every single foe.

Never mind, though, that such foemen plot, so persistently, the females' grace-less fall.

As they, almost, nev'r want to see the females up and about—or, on the damn go.

Oh! No! The foemen wouldn't dare dream of them ev'r being ingenious, industrious, or influential—and, tantalizingly tall.

True, all over again, that the females usually nev'r fall.

But, instead, they just stand steadily tall; and then pound right down any digressive, regressive, repressive, oppressive, or depressive, or even successive wall.

That's right, for the females have been taught to always fight right back!

Fight, right—back, mightily, and especially, when the fantastically fallible foemen—or, the mortal maulers are out to maul.

OH, NO! The Females aren't about to get whacked or be out of whack!

As their roundly righteous rise depends upon them staying well in tact, and, not, at all,

In poor condition.

Because, their Rise and Shine—inextinguishable—or, ev'r-burning flame,

Can't and won't be taken down or worn down, ev'r, by any attrition—or, long-lasting

Friction!

HOOPLA! Or, HURRAY!

Afterword

Perhaps mixed poetry is best.

Particular poems can and do effectuate some particularly powerful poetry. I am speaking, mainly, of the difference between fixed and un-fixed poems. Once, again, the first is like a sonnet, (or rhymed). And, the second is like free verse, (or un-rhymed). The use of various kinds of rhymes, and, rhyme schemes, and, even, types of poems, within a fixed poem brings about two, main effects—or, form, and rhythm. Of course, there are almost certainly limits that are so encountered when creating such fixed poems; whose end words, (or end-rhymes), almost, always, have to rhyme, or have rhythm, somehow. Contrarily, free verse or even informal free verse affords a poet more latitude, poetically. Even if, it still conforms to basic metrical rules and structure. However, being able to use one's "poetic license," to some extent if not a great extent is of great import. To do so with most if not all available—poetic tools; in order, to effectuate a particular affect or effect, is truly what poeticizing is all about: Conveying thoughts and feelings either loftily or impassionately and imaginatively—so freely.

Furthermore, free verse poetry can be broken down, even, further—so to speak, right, to prose-poetry; whose context and content both need not be metrical, or metered, at all. Therefore, it may very well be that prose-poetry affords the most poetic freedom of all, rightly; to a poet in deviating from conventionally poetic laws and form; in order, to create a very constant affect and/or final effect, poetically. Interestingly, such poetry, so very easily, encompasses some of poetry's most interesting, if not unique poems, and, even, poetic devices; right, in effectuating a very desirable affect and/or lasting effect: poems—catalog, confessional, narrative, riddle, and so on; devices—automatic writing, enjambment, meditation, stream-of-consciousness, and so forth. In conclusion, I have so spoken of the main differences between fixed and un-fixed poems; whose very diverse attributes allow for great diversity in poetry. Afterwards, I even plan to try my own hand at some very different—or, mixed poetry, poeticizing, plainly, and, quite freely.

Reference

Woods, Susanne. *The Poems of Aemilia Lanyer. Salve Deus Rex Judaeorum.* New York; Oxford: Oxford University Press, Inc., 1993.